SENSATIONAL
SOUPS

EASY AS...123

SENSATIONAL SOUPS

JENI WRIGHT

MAIN
STREET
BOOKS

DOUBLEDAY

NEW YORK•LONDON•TORONTO•SYDNEY•AUCKLAND

A CARROLL & BROWN BOOK

Created and produced by
CARROLL & BROWN LIMITED
5 Lonsdale Road
London NW6 6RA

Art Director Chrissie Lloyd
Designer Paul Stradling

Food Stylist Eric Treuillé

Photography David Murray

Production Wendy Rogers

Published in the United States by DOUBLEDAY
A division of Bantam Doubleday Dell Publishing Group, Inc.
1540 Broadway
New York
New York 10036

MAIN STREET BOOKS, DOUBLEDAY, and the portrayal of a building
with a tree are trademarks of Doubleday, a division of Bantam
Doubleday Dell Publishing Group, Inc.

Library of Congress Cataloging-in-Publication Data

Wright, Jeni.
       Easy as 1, 2, 3 sensational soups / Jeni Wright. --1st ed.
           p.   cm.
       Includes Index
       ISBN 0-385-48199-3
       1. Soups.   2. Quick and easy cookery I. Title.
       TX757.W75   1996
       641.8'13 -- dc20   95-37087
                                     CIP

Reproduced by Colourscan, Singapore

Printed and bound in England by Butler and Tanner Ltd

First American Edition: November 1996

Cover design Chrissie Lloyd
Cover photography David Murray

For my children, Oliver and Sophie

Sensational Soups

Contents

Rich and creamy, hot and spicy, cool and refreshing, even fruity, soups are as varied as they are versatile.

In this collection of fifty fabulous recipes there are soups to suit every occasion and every palate. Elegant first courses, nourishing main courses, soups from around the world, and soups for family meals as well as for informal and formal entertaining – all of them are simple to make in just three steps, using fresh, easy-to-find ingredients.

Tips and tricks of the trade are included too, together with clever ideas for garnishes and accompaniments to make your soups both look and taste simply sensational.

STOCKS

The basis of most soups is a good stock. Cubes and cans are convenient and quick, but nothing beats the full flavor of homemade stock, and you will find it makes a huge difference to the taste of your soups.

BEEF STOCK

Makes about 1½ qts

1 lb stewing beef, cut into pieces

1 lb beef bones, chopped

1 onion, studded with a few cloves

2 carrots, roughly chopped

2 celery stalks, roughly chopped

1 bouquet garni

Salt and freshly ground pepper

Brown the meat and bones in a preheated 425°F oven for about 30 minutes. Transfer to a pot and add the remaining ingredients and 2 qts water. Bring to a boil, half cover, and simmer for 4–5 hours. Strain, cool, and remove fat.

FISH STOCK

Makes about 1 qt

1½ lbs fish bones and trimmings

1 onion, quartered

Juice of ½ lemon

A few parsley sprigs

Salt and freshly ground pepper

Put all the ingredients in a large pot. Add 1½ qts water and bring to a boil. Half cover and simmer for 20 minutes, then strain.

CHICKEN STOCK

Makes about 1½ qts

1 chicken carcass, raw or cooked

Chicken giblets (except liver)

2 celery stalks, roughly chopped

2 carrots, roughly chopped

1 leek, roughly chopped

1 bouquet garni

Salt and freshly ground pepper

Break up the carcass and place in a large pot with the remaining ingredients and 2 qts water. Bring to a boil, half cover, and simmer for 3 hours. Strain, cool, and remove fat.

VEGETABLE STOCK

Makes about 2 qts

¾ lb mixed vegetables and trimmings (carrots, turnips, parsnips, celery, or leeks), chopped

1 onion, roughly chopped

2 bay leaves, torn

Salt and freshly ground pepper

Put all the ingredients in a large pot. Add 2½ qts water and bring to a boil. Simmer, uncovered, for 1 hour, then strain.

DASHI

This seaweed stock is used in Japanese soups. Instant dashi can be bought at supermarkets, or you can make your own.

Bring 1 oz kombu seaweed slowly to a boil in 1 qt water. Remove the seaweed. Add 1 oz dried bonito flakes and bring to a boil. Remove from the heat, and let the flakes settle.

Strain the liquid through cheesecloth into a clean pan and simmer for 10 minutes to concentrate the flavor.

CHICKEN NOODLE SOUP

With the addition of a few simple ingredients, fresh chicken stock is quickly transformed into a delicious nourishing homemade soup.

Serves 4–6

½–¾ lb boneless cooked chicken	¼ cup dry sherry
¼ lb spaghetti or other pasta	1 tsp chopped fresh thyme
1½ qts chicken stock	Salt and freshly ground pepper
4 ripe tomatoes, peeled, seeded, and chopped	

Special touches
Add ½ lb thinly sliced mushrooms with the tomatoes in step 2.

1 Cut the chicken into bite-size pieces, discarding any skin. Break the spaghetti into short lengths. Pour the chicken stock into a large pot and bring to a boil.

2 Add the broken spaghetti and the tomatoes and stir well to mix. Simmer, uncovered, for about 10 minutes, stirring once or twice, until the spaghetti is al dente (tender but firm to the bite).

3 Add the sherry and thyme and stir well, then add the chicken pieces and simmer for about 5 minutes until heated through. Add salt and pepper to taste. Serve hot in warmed bowls.

TOMATO BISQUE

This elegant looking soup is best made in summer with vine-ripened tomatoes for their intense flavor and color. Serve with dainty triangles of Melba toast (page 35) or thin slices of hot buttered toast.

Serves 4–6

2 tbs butter	½ cup dry white wine
1 tb canola oil	3 cups chicken or vegetable stock
1 onion, finely chopped	½ tsp sugar
1 tb all-purpose flour	Salt and freshly ground pepper
2 tbs tomato paste	¼ cup brandy
2 lbs ripe tomatoes, quartered	½ cup heavy cream

Special touches
¼ cup shredded fresh basil leaves (page 94) can be added with the brandy and cream in step 3.

BISQUE

Traditionally a bisque is made of seafood cooked with white wine, tomato paste, cream, and brandy. The shells of the seafood – usually crab or lobster – are pounded and strained to obtain a velvety smooth consistency. In this recipe, tomatoes are used in the same way as shellfish, but they are far less work – and the end result is just as good. If you want to make a shellfish bisque, substitute 1 lb crab or lobster in the shell for the tomatoes, and proceed as directed.

1 Melt the butter with the oil in a large pan, add the onion, and cook gently for 5 minutes or until soft. Sprinkle in the flour and add the tomato paste, then stir for 1–2 minutes to cook the flour.

2 Add the tomatoes and wine and bring to a boil. Add the stock, sugar, and salt and pepper to taste. Cover and simmer gently, stirring occasionally, for about 20 minutes.

3 Work the soup in a blender or food processor, then work through a strainer into a clean pan. Stir in the brandy and half the cream, and heat through. Taste for seasoning. Serve hot, garnished with the remaining cream.

CREAM OF MUSHROOM SOUP

Rich and earthy tasting, this superb soup gets its hearty flavor from the combination of both fresh and dried mushrooms. Beef stock is essential to augment the meaty flavor. Serve with hot, crusty Italian bread and fruity olive oil for dipping.

Serves 4

¾–1 lb fresh white mushrooms	1 qt hot beef stock
1 oz dried mushrooms (see box, right)	½ tsp dried thyme
3 tbs virgin olive oil	Salt and freshly ground pepper
2 shallots, roughly chopped	¼–½ cup heavy cream
1 garlic clove, roughly chopped	Chopped fresh parsley for garnish

DRIED MUSHROOMS

*Among the many kinds of dried mushroom are the French **morels** and Italian **porcini** or **boletus**, both of which are suitable for this soup. They are expensive, but their flavor is so intense that only a very small quantity is needed. Before use, soak them in about 1 cup warm water for about 20 minutes, then drain them, and reserve the soaking liquid to add extra flavor to the soup.*

1 Roughly chop the fresh mushrooms. Drain the dried mushrooms, reserving the soaking liquid, and roughly chop them. Heat the oil in a large pan and add the shallots and garlic. Cook gently, stirring frequently, for 5 minutes or until softened.

2 Add both types of mushroom and stir over moderate heat for 5 minutes or until they release their juices. Add the stock and soaking liquid and bring to a boil, stirring. Add the thyme and salt and pepper to taste, cover, and simmer gently for 30 minutes.

3 Ladle about three-quarters of the soup into a blender or food processor and work until smooth. Pour back into the pan and stir to mix. Stir in cream to taste, and taste for seasoning. Serve hot, sprinkled with parsley.

CARAMELIZED THREE ONION SOUP

Three members of the onion family – white onion, leeks, and shallots – are cooked together in this delicious soup. The idea of caramelizing onions to make a very rich, sweet-tasting soup is a French one, and it is unbelievably good.

MADEIRA

A fortified wine from the Portuguese island of the same name, Madeira is most often thought of as a drink, though it is also a useful flavoring ingredient in sweet and savory dishes. There are many varieties, from the dry, pale Sercial which is drunk as an aperitif, to the sweet, dark Malmsey, famous as an after-dinner drink. In this recipe, use dry or sweet Madeira, or port or sherry can be substituted.

Serves 4–6

6 tbs butter	1¼ qts hot chicken or vegetable stock
1 large white onion, finely chopped	Salt and freshly ground pepper
2 medium leeks, thinly sliced	¼ cup Madeira (see box, right)
4 shallots, finely chopped	½ cup crème fraîche (page 39) and a sprinkling of paprika for garnish
3 tbs dark brown sugar	
2 tbs all-purpose flour	

1 Melt the butter in a large heavy pan, add the onion, leeks, shallots, and sugar and cook over moderate to high heat, stirring all the time, until sticky and caramel-brown. This takes about 15 minutes. Remove from the heat.

2 Stir in the flour, then gradually add the stock, stirring well after each addition. Return to the heat and bring to a boil, stirring, then add salt and pepper to taste. Cover and simmer gently, stirring occasionally, for 20 minutes.

3 Work the soup in a blender or food processor until smooth, then return to a clean pan and reheat until bubbling. Add the Madeira, then taste and adjust seasoning. Serve hot, garnished with crème fraîche and paprika.

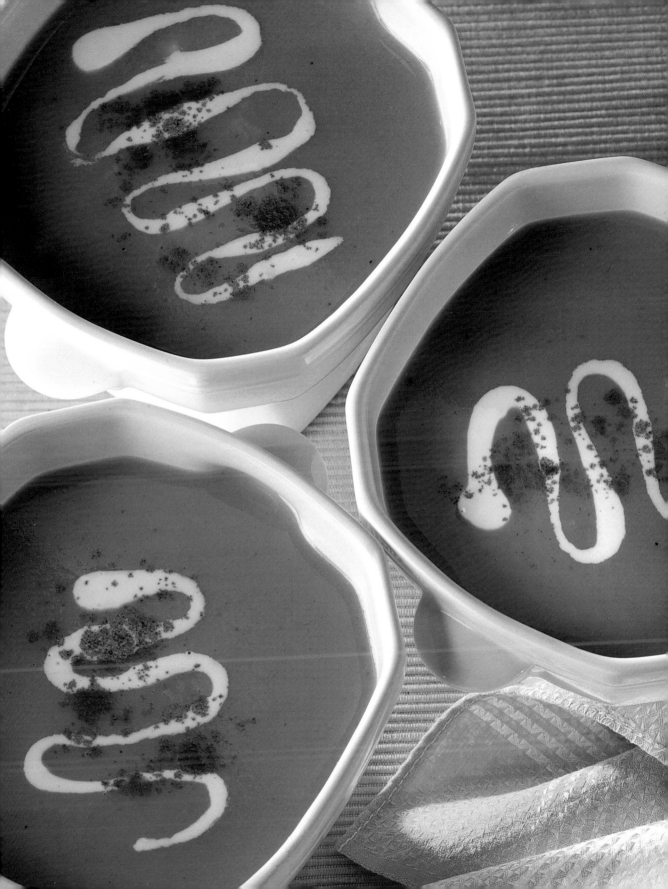

CAULIFLOWER AND CHEESE SOUP

Rich and creamy, this winter soup is warming and delicious with tangy mustard croûtes served on the side. Use a sharp Cheddar cheese so the finished soup has a mellow flavor and good color.

Serves 4

2 tbs butter	Salt and freshly ground pepper
1 onion, finely chopped	2 cups grated Cheddar cheese
1 medium cauliflower, weighing 1–1½ lbs, broken into florets	2 tsps Dijon-style mustard
2 tbs all-purpose flour	¼ tsp cayenne pepper for garnish
3 cups hot chicken or vegetable stock	Mustard croûtes (see box, right) for serving
3 cups milk	

MUSTARD CROUTES

With a wooden spoon, beat together ¼ cup softened butter, 2 tsps Dijon-style mustard, and salt and freshly ground pepper to taste. Cut 1 French baguette into ½-inch slices on the diagonal, discarding the ends. Arrange the slices on a baking sheet and toast them under a hot broiler for 2–3 minutes until golden brown on one side. Turn the slices over and spread the untoasted sides with the mustard butter. Return to the broiler and broil for another 2–3 minutes until the butter is melted and bubbling. If you like, sprinkle the mustard butter with a little cayenne pepper just before serving.

1 Melt the butter in a large pan and add the onion. Cook gently, stirring frequently, for 5 minutes or until softened. Add the cauliflower and toss to mix, then sprinkle in the flour and cook for 1–2 minutes, stirring constantly.

2 Gradually stir in the stock and 2 cups milk and bring to a boil. Add salt and pepper to taste, cover, and simmer for 15–20 minutes until the cauliflower is tender. Work in a blender or food processor until smooth.

3 Work through a strainer into a clean pan, add the remaining milk, three-quarters of the cheese, and the mustard, and reheat gently. Taste for seasoning. Serve hot, sprinkled with the remaining cheese and the cayenne, with the croûtes alongside.

CREAM OF WATERCRESS SOUP

Brilliant green watercress soup has a wonderful peppery bite. This recipe calls for very little cooking, which is why the finished soup looks so bright and fresh. The cream garnish, a clever little trick of the trade, gives the perfect finishing touch.

Serves 4

1 bunch watercress, weighing about ¼ lb	1 cup heavy cream
1 vegetable stock cube	Salt and freshly ground pepper
1 heaping tb all-purpose flour	

Special touches
For extra flavor, add a few chopped scallions or 1–2 roughly chopped garlic cloves in step 1.

1 Trim off any discolored leaves from the watercress and discard. Roughly chop the watercress leaves and stems. Place in a blender or food processor, and add 2 cups cold water, the stock cube, and the flour. Work until the watercress is very finely chopped.

2 Pour the contents of the blender or food processor into a large pan and add ⅔ cup cream and salt and pepper to taste. Bring to a boil over moderate heat, stirring constantly, then simmer for about 2 minutes.

3 Taste the soup for seasoning, then pour into warmed bowls. Drip the remaining cream from the tip of a teaspoon to form a circle on each serving of soup. Draw the tip of a knife through each drop to form heart shapes. Serve at once.

CURRIED PARSNIP SOUP

With its warm golden-yellow hue and rich and spicy flavor, this is the perfect soup to cheer up a cold winter's day. Serve with cheese-topped croûtes for a hearty first course.

Serves 4–6

2 tbs butter	3 cups hot chicken or vegetable stock
1 tb canola oil	
1 onion, roughly chopped	Salt and freshly ground pepper
2 tsps curry powder	2–2½ cups milk
½ tsp turmeric	Red-skinned apple slices for garnish
1 lb parsnips, thinly sliced	Cheese-topped croûtes (see box, right) for serving
1 Golden Delicious apple, chopped	

Special touches
Swirl in ½ cup plain yogurt or light cream just before serving.

CHEESE-TOPPED CROUTES

These crunchy baguette slices topped with melted cheese taste good with most vegetable soups. Cut 1 French baguette diagonally into slices about ½-inch thick, discarding the ends. Toast on one side only under a hot broiler for about 2 minutes until light golden. Turn the bread slices over so they are untoasted-side up, lightly spread with butter, and sprinkle with salt and black pepper to taste. Sprinkle 1 cup grated sharp Cheddar cheese evenly over the bread and return to the hot broiler for 2–3 minutes until the cheese is melted and bubbling. Serve hot.

1 Melt the butter with the oil in a large pan, add the onion, and sprinkle in the curry powder and turmeric. Cook gently, stirring constantly, for 2–3 minutes until the onion begins to soften and the spices smell fragrant.

2 Add the parsnips and apple and stir well to mix. Pour in the stock and bring to a boil. Add salt and pepper to taste. Cover the pan and simmer gently, stirring occasionally, for 30 minutes or until the parsnips are very tender.

3 Work the soup in a blender or food processor until smooth, then return to a clean pan, and stir in 2 cups milk. Reheat, and add more milk for a thinner soup if you like. Taste for seasoning. Serve hot, garnished with apple slices, with the croûtes alongside.

THAI SPINACH AND COCONUT SOUP

Spicy hot Thai ingredients are cooled down with coconut milk to make a refreshing soup with just a hint of seafood.

Serves 4–6

1 stalk lemon grass	14-oz can coconut milk
4–8 raw shrimp, peeled and deveined	2½ cups hot chicken or fish stock
2 shallots, roughly chopped	1–2 tbs Thai fish sauce
2 garlic cloves, roughly chopped	1 tsp sugar
2 red bird's eye chilies, seeded and roughly chopped	4–6 ozs fresh spinach leaves
Juice of 1 lime	¼ cup toasted coconut (see box, right) for serving
2 tbs canola oil	

COCONUT

Freshly shredded coconut and coconut milk are favorite ingredients of Thai cooks. Toasted coconut is often used as a garnish. It is particularly appropriate with the coconut milk in this recipe, because it makes a crisp contrast to the soft textures of the soup itself. To toast coconut to use as a garnish, spread ¼ cup shredded coconut on a baking sheet and toast in a preheated 375°F oven for 5 minutes, stirring the coconut once or twice.

1 Roughly chop the lemon grass and shrimp, and place in a food processor with the shallots, garlic, chilies, and lime juice. Work to a wet paste. Heat the oil in a wok, add the paste, and stir-fry for 5 minutes until dry and fragrant.

2 Pour the coconut milk into the wok, add the stock, and stir vigorously to combine with the paste. Bring to a boil, then add 1 tb fish sauce and the sugar. Simmer gently, stirring occasionally, while preparing the spinach.

3 Stack the spinach leaves, roll up, and cut crosswise into shreds. Add the shreds to the wok and simmer for 3–5 minutes until wilted. Taste, and add more fish sauce if you like. Serve hot, sprinkled with toasted coconut.

JERUSALEM ARTICHOKE AND TOMATO SOUP

This warming, earthy tasting soup is full of nutritious ingredients for a cold winter's day. With its festive coloring, it also makes a great holiday soup.

Serves 4–6

2 tbs virgin olive oil	1 heaping tb all-purpose flour
1 onion, finely chopped	14-oz can peeled plum tomatoes
1 lb Jerusalem artichokes, peeled and sliced	About 1¼ qts hot chicken or vegetable stock
Juice of ½ lemon	1 tsp dried basil or oregano
2 garlic cloves, chopped	Salt and freshly ground pepper

Finishing touches
Add the finely grated zest and juice of ½ orange and ½ cup light cream in step 3.

JERUSALEM ARTICHOKES

*These knobbly looking vegetables have a bad reputation for being quite difficult to peel, but look for the new varieties appearing in the market – these are straighter and therefore far less time-consuming to prepare. The name Jerusalem artichoke is misleading because the vegetable has nothing to do with the city of Jerusalem or with globe artichokes, but it is derived from the Italian word **girasole**, meaning sunflower, which is a related plant. Now often referred to simply as sunchokes, Jerusalem artichokes are a rich source of iron and other minerals, as well as calcium and vitamin C.*

1 Heat the oil in a large pan, add the onion, and cook gently for 5 minutes or until softened. Add the artichokes, lemon juice, and garlic and cook for 5 minutes, then sprinkle in the flour and stir over moderate heat for 1 minute.

2 Add the tomatoes and break up with a wooden spoon, then add 1¼ qts stock and bring to a boil. Add the herbs, and salt and pepper to taste. Cover and simmer gently for 25 minutes or until the artichokes are tender.

3 Work the soup in a blender or food processor, then heat through in a clean pan. Stir in more stock if the consistency of the soup is too thick. Taste for seasoning. Serve hot, garnished generously with black pepper.

CREAM OF PUMPKIN SOUP

Smooth as silk, this golden pumpkin soup looks spectacular when served in a large white tureen as illustrated here, but for Halloween you may want to serve it in the pumpkin shell – see the box on the right for directions on how to do it.

Serves 4

1 tb butter	1 garlic clove, roughly chopped
2 tbs canola oil	1½ tsps ground ginger
1 onion, roughly chopped	1 qt chicken or vegetable stock
4-lb pumpkin, cut into chunks (see box, right)	Salt and freshly ground pepper
2 potatoes, peeled and diced	1 cup heavy cream

PUMPKIN

If the soup is not being served in the shell, prepare the pumpkin by cutting it into eighths, scraping off the seeds and threads, cutting off the skin, and slicing the flesh into chunks. If serving the soup in the shell, cut a thick slice off the top of the pumpkin and reserve for the lid. Scrape out the seeds and threads, then cut away the flesh from inside. Heat the shell in a 300°F oven for about 10 minutes before using.

1 Melt the butter with the oil in a large pan, and add the onion, pumpkin, and potatoes. Cook gently, stirring frequently, for about 5 minutes. Add the garlic and ginger and stir for 1–2 minutes.

2 Pour in the stock and bring to a boil, then add salt and pepper to taste. Cover and simmer gently, stirring occasionally, for 30 minutes or until the vegetables are very tender.

3 Work the soup in a blender or food processor until smooth, then pour through a strainer into a clean pan. Add two-thirds of the cream and heat through. Taste for seasoning. Serve hot, swirled with the remaining cream.

CHILLED SOUPS

For those lazy, hazy days of summer, when cooking is a chore, chilled soups that require no cooking are the perfect choice. For an *al fresco* barbecue, serve them in tureens with ice cubes floating on top.

GAZPACHO

Serves 4–6

2 large green bell peppers, cored and seeded

1 large cucumber

2 lbs ripe tomatoes

1 Spanish onion

2 garlic cloves

2 15-oz cans tomato juice

⅓ cup extra-virgin olive oil

⅓ cup red wine vinegar

2 tbs tomato paste

Salt and freshly ground pepper

Parsley ice cubes (see box, right) for serving

1 Roughly chop the peppers, cucumber, tomatoes, onion, and garlic. Work in batches in a food processor until finely chopped.

2 Work the vegetables through a strainer into a bowl and stir in the remaining ingredients, adding salt and pepper to taste.

3 Work in batches again in the food processor, then strain into a tureen. Cover and chill for at least 4 hours. Stir well and taste for seasoning, then add a few parsley ice cubes. Serve at once.

TZATZIKI SOUP

Serves 4–6

1 large cucumber, washed

2 garlic cloves, finely chopped

2 tbs white wine vinegar

Salt and freshly ground pepper

2 cups plain low-fat yogurt

About 1 cup cold chicken or vegetable stock

2 tbs chopped fresh mint

4–6 cooked large shrimp, peeled and chopped

Mint ice cubes (see box, right) for serving

1 Grate the cucumber, including the peel, into a bowl. Add the garlic, wine vinegar, and salt and pepper to taste.

2 Slowly whisk in the yogurt until evenly combined, then add enough stock to give a pouring consistency. Cover and chill for at least 4 hours.

3 Stir the chopped mint into the soup, taste for seasoning, and add a little more stock if the soup is too thick. Serve at once, topped with the shrimp and a few mint ice cubes.

HERB ICE CUBES

A chilled soup keeps cool if you float ice cubes in it just before serving. These cubes are set with fresh herbs.

Half fill ice cube trays with cold water. Select fresh herb sprigs and pull off small, well-shaped leaves. Place 1 herb leaf in each of the ice cube sections and place in the freezer until just frozen.

Pour in enough water to cover the herb leaves and return to the freezer until solid.

APPLE AND ALMOND CREAM SOUP

With its brilliant sunshine-yellow color, this is the perfect soup to brighten up a cold gray day. The combination of apple and onion gives a piquant sweet flavor, with just a hint of spice from the golden saffron threads.

Serves 4

1½ lbs Golden Delicious apples	Pinch of saffron threads (see box, right)
¼ cup butter	Salt and freshly ground pepper
1 onion, finely chopped	½ cup light cream
6 tbs ground almonds	Toasted sliced almonds (page 94) and saffron threads for garnish
About 3½ cups hot chicken or vegetable stock	

SAFFRON

The most expensive spice in the world, saffron threads are the stigmas of the small purple crocus flower. They are expensive because there are only three stigmas to each flower, and each one is picked by hand. Saffron threads are pungent in flavor, so a little goes a long way, and a pinch will color a dish a beautiful bright yellow. Saffron powder can be used instead of threads; it is less expensive, but its flavor isn't as good.

1 Cut the apples into quarters and remove the cores, then roughly chop the apples. Melt the butter in a large pan, add the onion, and cook gently for about 5 minutes until softened. Add the apples and cook gently, stirring, for 2–3 minutes.

2 Sprinkle in the ground almonds and stir to blend well for 1–2 minutes. Pour in 3½ cups stock and bring to a boil, then add the saffron and salt and pepper to taste. Cover and simmer gently for 20 minutes or until the apples are tender.

3 Work the soup in a blender or food processor, then work through a strainer into a clean pan. Add the cream, reheat gently, and add a little stock if too thick. Taste for seasoning. Serve hot, topped with almonds and saffron.

EGGPLANT CAVIAR SOUP

If you like the Middle Eastern dip *baba ghanoush*, known in English as eggplant caviar, you'll love this soup. Heady with the strong flavors of broiled eggplant, garlic, and sesame seed paste, it is not a soup for the faint-hearted.

Serves 4–6

2 eggplant, total weight ¾–1 lb, halved lengthwise	4½–5 cups hot chicken or vegetable stock
Salt and freshly ground pepper	2 tbs Greek or other thick yogurt
About 1 tb virgin olive oil	1–2 tbs fresh lemon juice (optional)
2 garlic cloves, roughly chopped	Greek yogurt and chopped fresh coriander (cilantro) for garnish
1–2 tbs tahini paste (see box, right)	

Finishing touches
Serve with hot pita bread to round out the Middle Eastern theme.

TAHINI

*Sometimes called **tahina**, this is a thick, creamy paste made from toasted or untoasted white sesame seeds that are ground very fine until their natural oil is released – much the same process as making peanut butter. Tahini is widely used in Middle Eastern cooking as a dip or spread ingredient – hummus and baba ghanoush being two good examples. It is especially prized for its nutritional value – sesame seeds are packed with vitamins, minerals, calcium, iron, and protein. When combined with bread, tahini paste makes a complete protein, which is why hummus and pita bread are so often eaten together in the Middle East.*

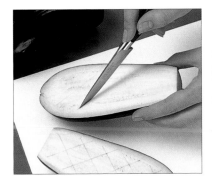

1 Score the eggplant flesh in a crosshatch pattern, sprinkle with salt, and let stand for 30 minutes. Rinse and pat dry, then brush with oil. Cook under a hot broiler, turning often, for about 10 minutes until the skins are blistered and the flesh charred.

2 Roughly chop the eggplant. If you prefer a milder soup, scoop the flesh out of the skins and discard the skins. Place the eggplant in a blender, add the garlic and tahini, and work to a purée. With the machine running, gradually add about half the stock.

3 Pour the purée and the remaining stock into a large pan and heat gently until hot. If too thick, stir in more stock. Stir in the 2 tbs yogurt. Season to taste, adding lemon juice and more tahini if you like. Serve hot, garnished with yogurt and chopped coriander.

CREAM OF BROCCOLI SOUP

This soup comes from Italy, where the unusual combination of broccoli, anchovies, and Parmesan cheese is a popular vegetable dish. Blend these ingredients together to make soup, and the result is smooth and creamy, with a delicious peppery bite.

Serves 4–6

¾ –1 lb broccoli	Freshly ground pepper
4 canned anchovies, roughly chopped	¾ cup light cream
5–5½ cups hot chicken or vegetable stock	Grated Parmesan cheese for garnish
¼ cup grated Parmesan cheese	Anchovy crostini (see box, right) for serving

ANCHOVY CROSTINI

Drain a 2-oz jar or can anchovy fillets in olive oil and mash the anchovies to a paste with a mortar and pestle with 1 finely chopped garlic clove, 1 tb virgin olive oil, 1 tsp red or white wine vinegar, and freshly ground black pepper to taste. Cut 8–12 ½-inch thick slices of Italian country-style bread and toast under a hot broiler for 2 minutes on each side or until golden. Brush with a little olive oil, then spread with the anchovy mixture. Serve at once, or heat through in a preheated 350°F oven for about 10 minutes. If you like, garnish each crostini with a parsley leaf just before serving.

1 Separate the broccoli florets and stems, chop the stems, and place them in a large pan with the anchovies and 5 cups stock. Bring to a boil, cover, and simmer for 15 minutes or until the stems are just tender.

2 Add the florets, ¼ cup Parmesan cheese, and plenty of pepper. Cover and continue to simmer for another 10 minutes or until the florets are tender. Transfer to a blender or food processor and work until smooth.

3 Reheat the soup in a clean pan. Stir in the cream and heat gently without boiling, stirring constantly. Taste for seasoning and add more stock if the soup is too thick. Serve hot, sprinkled with additional Parmesan, with the crostini alongside.

CREAM OF CRAB SOUP

Rich and creamy, with a delicate hint of the sea, this is the perfect first course for a summer dinner party. To complement its flavor and pretty pink color, serve it with chilled dry rosé or even pink Champagne.

Serves 4–6

1 lb ripe tomatoes	Salt and freshly ground pepper
2 tbs butter	10 ozs lump crabmeat
2 shallots, finely chopped	½ cup heavy cream
2 tbs all-purpose flour	Cayenne pepper and fresh dill sprigs for garnish
½ cup dry white wine	
3½–4 cups hot fish stock	Melba toast (see box, right) for serving
Few drops Tabasco sauce, or to taste	

1 Roughly chop the tomatoes. Melt the butter in a large pan and add the shallots. Cook gently, stirring, for about 5 minutes until softened. Add the tomatoes, flour, and wine, and stir well to mix. Pour in 3½ cups stock and bring to a boil, stirring.

2 Add Tabasco sauce and season to taste, cover, and simmer gently, stirring occasionally, for 15–20 minutes. Crumble about three-quarters of the crabmeat into the soup and heat through for 5 minutes. Purée the soup in a blender or food processor.

3 Work the soup through a strainer into a clean pan. Stir in the cream and heat through, adding more stock if too thick. Taste for seasoning. Serve hot, garnished with the remaining crab and the cayenne and dill, with the Melba toast alongside.

JAPANESE SOUPS

Pretty as a picture, Japanese soups are simple and elegant. There is little cooking involved, so the ingredients must speak for themselves. For this reason they should be the freshest and best you can find.

CLEAR SOUP WITH SHRIMP FLOWERS

Serves 4

4 raw jumbo shrimp

A little cornstarch for coating

Pinch salt

4 cups dashi (page 6)

1 tsp Japanese soy sauce

4 small watercress sprigs

1 Shell and devein the shrimp, leaving the tail shells intact. With a small, sharp knife, make a slit along the back of each shrimp and cut through to the other side. Push the tail through the slit so that it pokes out the other side.

2 Dip the shrimp in a little cornstarch mixed with the salt, and shake off any excess. Plunge the shrimp into a pan of simmering water and blanch for 1 minute. Lift out with a slotted spoon and pat dry with paper towels.

3 Bring the dashi to a boil in a saucepan, and stir in the soy sauce. Ladle into 4 soup bowls and float a shrimp and a watercress sprig on top of each one. Serve at once.

CLEAR SOUP WITH FLOWER BLOSSOMS

Serves 4

3–4 small carrots

1 thin daikon or Japanese white radish

4 cups dashi (page 6)

3 tbs white miso (Japanese bean paste)

3 tbs mirin (Japanese rice wine)

1 Peel the carrots, then cut vertical grooves around each one with a channel knife. Cut the carrots crosswise into very thin slices. Repeat with the daikon.

2 Bring the dashi to a boil in a saucepan. Put the miso in a bowl and pour in a little of the hot dashi. Whisk well to mix. Work the miso mixture through a fine strainer into the dashi in the pan, then stir in the mirin.

3 Add the carrot and daikon flowers and simmer gently without boiling for about 5 minutes until just tender. Ladle the soup into 4 bowls and serve at once.

MISO SOUP WITH TOFU AND SCALLIONS

Serves 4

½ lb firm tofu

1 small bunch scallions

4 cups dashi (page 6)

3 tbs red miso (Japanese bean paste)

1 Cut the tofu into small, even-sized cubes. Chop the scallions as finely as possible. Divide the tofu and scallions equally among 4 soup bowls.

2 Bring the dashi to a boil in a saucepan. Put the miso in a bowl and pour in a little of the hot dashi. Whisk well to mix.

3 Work the miso mixture through a fine strainer into the dashi in the pan, heat gently without boiling, then carefully ladle the dashi over the tofu and scallions. Serve at once.

FRENCH GREEN PEA SOUP WITH MINT

Shallots and lettuce add a unique French flavor to this fresh-tasting, minty pea soup. Make it in early summer when the new season's peas are young and sweet, or in winter with frozen peas – both are equally good.

Serves 4–6

1½ lbs fresh peas in their shells, or ¾ lb frozen peas	1 qt hot chicken or vegetable stock
¼ cup butter	1 tsp dried mint
2 large shallots, finely chopped	Large pinch sugar
About 1½ cups lettuce leaves, shredded	Salt and freshly ground pepper
2 tbs all-purpose flour	½ cup crème fraîche (see box, right)
	Tiny fresh mint leaves for garnish

CREME FRAICHE

This is the French for fresh cream, and although it is sometimes used in the same way as heavy cream it is not quite the same. Like a cross between sour cream and heavy cream, it has a rich and velvety consistency with a tangy, refreshing taste. It can be used in cooking because it contains at least 35% butterfat and does not curdle when heated; it also tastes good served chilled with fresh fruit and hot desserts. Look for it at gourmet markets, or make your own by mixing ½ cup heavy cream with 1 tb buttermilk and allowing it to stand at room temperature for 8 hours or until thick.

1 Shell the fresh peas. Melt the butter in a large pan, add the shallots, and cook gently for about 5 minutes until softened. Add the peas and lettuce and stir well, then cover and sweat gently for 10 minutes, stirring frequently.

2 Sprinkle in the flour and cook, stirring, for 1–2 minutes, then gradually add the stock and bring to a boil. Add the dried mint, sugar, and salt and pepper to taste, cover, and simmer for 10 minutes.

3 Work the soup in a blender or food processor, then work through a fine strainer into a clean pan. Discard the skins. Stir in the crème fraîche and heat through, then taste for seasoning. Serve hot, sprinkled with fresh mint.

TOMATO AND BASIL SOUP

Crushed sieved tomatoes give this soup its glorious deep red color. Made from pantry ingredients, it takes less than 30 minutes to prepare and cook.

Serves 4–6

2 tbs virgin olive oil	5–5½ cups hot chicken or vegetable stock
1 onion, finely chopped	
2 garlic cloves, finely chopped	Salt and freshly ground pepper
2 tbs bottled pesto	Shredded fresh basil (page 94) and coarsely ground black pepper for garnish
3 cups crushed sieved tomatoes (see box, right)	

Finishing touches

If you like, you can serve each bowl of soup with a small spoonful of pesto in the center, in which case omit the basil garnish.

CRUSHED SIEVED TOMATOES

*Called **passata** in Italian, crushed sieved tomatoes are available in bottles and cans at Italian delis and gourmet markets. As their name suggests, they are simply tomatoes that have been crushed then sieved to remove all of the skins and seeds. The end result is a fresh tasting, brilliant red smooth mixture, much less thick than a tomato paste. Passata is a natural convenience food, indispensable in the Italian kitchen. You will find that it takes most of the hard work out of making soups, stews, and tomato sauce for pizza and pasta.*

1 Heat the oil in a large pan, add the onion, garlic, and pesto, and cook gently, stirring frequently, for about 5 minutes until the onion has softened.

2 Add the tomatoes and 5 cups stock, stir well, and bring to a boil. Add salt and pepper to taste. Cover and simmer gently, stirring occasionally, for 15 minutes.

3 Blend the soup in the pan with a hand blender. Taste for seasoning and add more stock if too thick. Serve hot, sprinkled with basil and pepper.

VICHYSSOISE

Pale, creamy, and velvety smooth, this classic iced soup originated at the Ritz-Carlton Hotel in New York. Always served garnished with chives, it makes the most elegant of first courses.

Serves 6

6 medium leeks, total weight about 1¼ lbs	4½ cups chicken stock
¼ cup butter	1 cup light cream
Salt and freshly ground white pepper	Fresh chives for garnish
3 medium potatoes, total weight about 1¼ lbs	

Finishing touches

For a special dinner party, decorate each serving with an attractive pattern of cream (page 95) before garnishing with chives.

1 Trim off the root ends and dark green parts of the leeks, then thinly slice the white and light green parts. Wash the slices thoroughly. Melt the butter in a large pan and add the leeks and salt and pepper to taste.

2 Cook gently, stirring often, for 7–10 minutes until softened but not colored. Peel and thinly slice the potatoes and add to the pan. Add the stock and bring to a boil. Cover and simmer, stirring occasionally, for 30 minutes.

3 Work the soup in a blender or food processor, then work through a strainer into a clean pan. Stir in the cream, and let the soup cool. Chill for at least 4 hours, then taste for seasoning. Serve chilled, garnished with chives.

ZUCCHINI SOUP WITH BLUE CHEESE AND SAGE

Make this soup in late summer or early fall when zucchini are plentiful, and serve it with hot focaccia. The combination of blue cheese and sage, with just a hint of garlic, is truly wonderful. If the weather is warm, this soup is also delicious served chilled.

Serves 4–6

2 tbs canola oil	1 tsp dried sage
1 onion, roughly chopped	Salt and freshly ground pepper
2 garlic cloves, roughly chopped	¼ lb soft blue cheese (see box, right), rind removed and diced
2 lbs zucchini, roughly chopped	
2½ cups chicken or vegetable stock	⅔ cup heavy cream
1 cup milk	Fresh sage leaves for garnish

1 Heat the oil in a large pan and add the onion, garlic, and zucchini. Cook the vegetables over moderate heat, stirring frequently, for 10 minutes or until the water runs from the zucchini.

2 Add the stock and milk and bring to a boil. Add the sage and salt and pepper to taste. Cover and simmer for 20 minutes. Add the cheese and stir until melted. Work the soup in a blender or food processor until smooth.

3 Pour the soup through a strainer into a clean pan. Add the cream and reheat the soup gently, stirring all the time. Taste for seasoning. Serve hot, garnished with sage leaves.

SPICED CARROT AND ORANGE SOUP

This fresh-tasting soup has a hint of Indian spiciness. Warm naan bread is an ideal accompaniment, although pappadams would go equally well.

Serves 4

3 tbs canola oil	4–4½ cups hot chicken or vegetable stock
1 onion, roughly chopped	
1½ lbs carrots, thinly sliced	¼ cup orange juice
2–3 tsps ground coriander	Julienned orange zest and crushed coriander seeds for garnish
Salt and freshly ground pepper	

Seasonal choice
Use ½ lb celery or celery root and only 1 lb carrots, and stir in ½ cup light cream just before serving.

CORIANDER

*Both the seeds and the leaves of this aromatic herb have been used in kitchens around the world for many, many years. It's interesting to note, however, that their flavors differ greatly. Whole coriander seeds and ground coriander powder are quite commonly used in Indian cooking, especially in the making of curry powders and curry pastes, **garam masalas**, and chutneys and pickles. They are bittersweet, with a subtle hint of orange peel. Fresh coriander leaves, known as cilantro, typically flavor the cuisines of Mexico and Asia. They have quite a pungent flavor, which some say is reminiscent of anise.*

1 Heat the oil in a large pan, add the onion, and cook gently for 5 minutes until soft. Add the carrots, coriander, and salt and pepper to taste. Cover and sweat the carrots gently for 5 minutes. Shake the pan from time to time.

2 Pour in 4 cups stock and bring to a boil. Cover the pan and simmer gently, stirring occasionally, for 30 minutes or until the carrots feel very soft when pierced. Work in a blender or food processor until smooth.

3 Work through a strainer into a clean pan. Add the orange juice and reheat, adding more stock if the soup is too thick. Taste for seasoning. Serve hot, garnished with orange zest and a sprinkling of crushed coriander seeds.

CURRIED TURKEY SOUP

This soup is perfect for using up leftover turkey and vegetables after Thanksgiving or Christmas. For a hearty supper, serve with cheese-topped croûtes (page 19).

Serves 4–6

2 tbs canola oil	2 tbs all-purpose flour
1 large onion, finely chopped	1½ qts hot turkey stock
4 celery stalks, thinly sliced	Salt and freshly ground pepper
2 lbs mixed root vegetables (parsnips, carrots, and turnip), diced	2 cups diced cooked turkey meat
2 tbs curry powder	Celery leaves for garnish

CURRY POWDER

There are many different blends of Indian spices labeled "curry powder," but the best one to buy is called **garam masala**. *This is a high quality blend of different ground spices that varies according to individual brands. Most garam masalas are made up of coriander, mustard, and fenugreek seeds, together with chilies, ginger, pepper, and turmeric. Sometimes they are scented with cloves, cinnamon, and nutmeg. It's worth experimenting with different brands to find the one you like best, or you can make your own by grinding the spices of your choice in an electric grinder or with a mortar and pestle.*

1 Heat the oil in a large pan and add the onion and celery. Cook gently for 5 minutes or until softened. Add the root vegetables, sprinkle in the curry powder and flour, and stir for 1–2 minutes.

2 Pour in the stock, bring to a boil, and add salt and pepper to taste. Cover and simmer for 15–20 minutes until the root vegetables are tender.

3 Add the diced turkey meat to the soup and simmer gently, stirring occasionally, for about 5 minutes until heated through. Taste for seasoning. Serve hot, garnished with celery leaves.

HAM AND CORN CHOWDER

Rich and creamy, this New England style chowder uses ham and yellow corn rather than clams, which makes it a great everyday soup all the family will enjoy.

Serves 4

1 tb butter	1 bay leaf
2 tbs canola oil	Salt and freshly ground pepper
1 onion, finely chopped	1 cup milk
2 small bell peppers (1 green and 1 red), cored, seeded, and diced	11-oz can yellow corn, drained
2 tbs all-purpose flour	¼ lb thick-sliced cooked ham, diced
1 lb potatoes, peeled and diced	½ cup light cream
3 cups hot chicken stock	Paprika for garnish

CHOWDER

*The American chowder comes from the French **chaudière**, a cauldron used by French fishermen to make fish stews with their catch. Original chowders were always made with fish, the most famous ones being clam chowders (page 71). Nowadays, any thick soup containing chunky vegetables, meat, poultry, or fish can be called a chowder, but the rule is that New England recipes are creamy, and Manhattan-style chowders are tomato-based.*

1 Melt the butter with the oil in a large pan and add the onion and peppers. Cook over gentle heat for about 5 minutes until the vegetables are softened. Sprinkle in the flour and stir for 1–2 minutes.

2 Add the potatoes, then pour in the stock and bring to a boil. Add the bay leaf and salt and pepper to taste, cover, and simmer gently for 20 minutes or until the potatoes are very soft.

3 Stir in the milk, then add the corn and ham and heat through for about 5 minutes. Remove the bay leaf. Stir in the cream and taste for seasoning. Serve hot, sprinkled with paprika.

ISLAND CRAB AND SPINACH SOUP

Based on the Caribbean soup, *callaloo*, this soup is rich with coconut milk and spicy with chili powder and hot pepper sauce. In the Caribbean it is served fiery hot, but you can add as little or as much spice as you like.

Serves 4

¼ lb okra	1 cup canned coconut milk
2 tbs butter	1 tsp dried thyme
1 tb canola oil	Salt and freshly ground pepper
4 scallions, finely chopped	½ lb fresh spinach, shredded
2 garlic cloves, finely chopped	10 ozs lump crabmeat
1 tsp hot chili powder	Tabasco sauce
1¼ qts hot fish or chicken stock	Cayenne pepper for garnish

CALLALOO

Each island in the Caribbean has its own version of callaloo, based on okra, leafy green vegetables, coconut milk, and spices. This crab version is one of the most popular. Others include salt pork or bacon, and some are completely vegetarian.

*The local leafy greens for callaloo are taro leaves, which islanders call by their nicknames – **dasheen** or callaloo leaves. Outside the Caribbean, fresh spinach is the best substitute.*

1 Thinly slice the okra. Heat the butter and oil in a large pan, add the scallions, and cook gently for 5 minutes until softened. Add the okra, garlic, and chili powder and stir for 1–2 minutes.

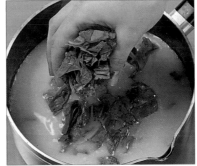

2 Pour in the stock and coconut milk and bring to a boil. Add the thyme and salt and pepper to taste, then the shredded spinach. Cover and simmer for 20 minutes, stirring occasionally.

3 Add the crabmeat and heat through for about 5 minutes. Taste for seasoning and add Tabasco to taste. Serve at once, sprinkled with cayenne.

GOULASH SOUP

In Hungary and Austria, goulash is served as both a stew and a soup, depending on the occasion. Here, boiled potatoes are served as an accompaniment for a hearty meal, but dumplings are equally traditional.

Serves 6

2 tbs canola oil	1¼ qts hot beef stock
2 large onions, thinly sliced	½ tsp dried marjoram
1 garlic clove, finely chopped	¼ tsp caraway seeds
2 tsps paprika	Salt and freshly ground pepper
1 lb boneless beef shank, diced small	Boiled potatoes and finely chopped fresh parsley for serving
2 tbs tomato paste	

Finishing touches
For a lighter meal, omit the potatoes and serve topped with spoonfuls of sour cream and a liberal sprinkling of paprika.

POTATO DUMPLINGS

Cook 1 lb potatoes in boiling salted water for 20 minutes or until tender; drain, and mash. Add ½ cup all-purpose flour, 1 beaten egg, and 1 tsp caraway seeds, and mix with your hands. Turn out onto a floured surface and knead to form a soft, smooth dough, adding more flour if the dough is too sticky. Divide the dough in half and form each half into a cylinder shape. Cut each cylinder into 9 equal pieces and roll into balls. Drop the dumplings into a large pan of boiling salted water and cook for 1–2 minutes until they rise to the surface. Drain them well and add to the soup just before serving.

1 Heat the oil in a large pan and add the onions, garlic, and paprika. Cook gently, stirring frequently, for about 10 minutes until the onions are softened and pale golden in color.

2 Add the meat, increase the heat to moderate, and cook, stirring constantly, until the meat is browned on all sides. Add the tomato paste and stir for 1–2 minutes, then pour in the stock and bring to a boil.

3 Lower the heat, add the marjoram, caraway seeds, and salt and pepper to taste. Cover and simmer for 1½ hours or until the meat is tender. Taste for seasoning. Serve at once, with the potatoes and parsley.

BOUILLABAISSE

This famous fish soup from Marseille on the Mediterranean is traditionally made with local rock fish. Outside the area it can be made with grouper, mackerel, or eel – or any similar white and oily fish that is in season.

Serves 4

¼ cup virgin olive oil	1½ qts hot fish or chicken stock
1 onion, thinly sliced	Pinch saffron threads (page 28)
2 leeks, thinly sliced	1 medium strip orange zest
1 small fennel bulb, thinly sliced	1 bouquet garni
2–3 garlic cloves, minced	Salt and freshly ground pepper
4 tomatoes, peeled, seeded, and chopped	3 lbs mixed white and oily fish, including bones
1 tb tomato paste	About 2 tbs Pernod (optional)
1 cup dry white wine	Rouille (see box, right) for serving

ROUILLE

This is the fiery hot chili mayonnaise that is always served with bouillabaisse in the south of France. It can be spooned into individual servings, or spread on slices of crisp hot toast and served separately. To make rouille, work ½ cup mayonnaise in a blender or food processor with 1 bird's eye chili, seeded and roughly chopped, 4 garlic cloves, roughly chopped, 1 tb tomato paste, and ½ tsp salt. Keep in the refrigerator until ready to serve.

1 Heat the oil in a large pan and add the onion, leeks, fennel, and garlic to taste. Cook over moderate heat, stirring frequently, for about 10 minutes until the vegetables are softened but not colored. Add the tomatoes, tomato paste, and wine and stir well.

2 Add the stock, saffron, orange zest, bouquet garni, and salt and pepper to taste and bring to a rapid boil. Partially cover the pan and let the liquid bubble gently for about 30 minutes, stirring occasionally, until reduced slightly.

3 Cut the fish into chunks. Remove the orange zest and bouquet garni from the soup, and add the firm fish. Simmer for 5 minutes, add the delicate fish, and simmer for 2–3 minutes. Stir in the Pernod, if using, and taste for seasoning. Serve hot, with rouille.

FRENCH ONION SOUP

Made famous at Les Halles, the fruit and vegetable market in Paris, this hearty soup makes a warming winter lunch or supper. Serve it in true bistro style – with a crusty baguette, slices of French cheese and sausage, and a bottle of red wine.

Serves 4

2 tbs butter	2 tbs all-purpose flour
1 tb virgin olive oil	6 cups hot beef stock
1½ lbs onions, thinly sliced	¼ cup brandy
1 tsp sugar	4 slices French baguette, toasted
Salt and freshly ground pepper	¼ lb Gruyère cheese, grated
½ cup dry red wine	

Special touches
Spread the toasted baguette slices with a little Dijon-style mustard or rub with the cut side of a peeled and halved garlic clove.

LES HALLES

This huge wholesale fruit and vegetable market used to be in the center of Paris until 1969, when it was moved to Rungis on the outskirts of the city. It was renowned for its brasseries and bars where market porters would stop on their way home after a night's work and revive themselves with bowls of steaming hot onion soup topped with toasted bread and cheese. Party-goers too would often end up at Les Halles in the early hours of the morning, staving off their hangovers with this famous soup. Today, although the market has moved outside of Paris, **soupe à l'oignon gratinée** *remains a firm favorite in Parisian bistros.*

1 Melt the butter with the oil in a large heavy pan and add the onions, sugar, and salt and pepper to taste. Cover with waxed paper and cook over very gentle heat, stirring frequently, for about 20 minutes until golden brown.

2 Add the wine and stir over moderate heat for 5 minutes or until the onions are glazed. Sprinkle in the flour and stir for 1–2 minutes, then stir in the stock. Bring to a boil, cover, and simmer for 30 minutes. Taste for seasoning.

3 Divide the soup among 4 heatproof bowls, stir 1 tb brandy into each, and top with a slice of toast. Sprinkle with the cheese and place under a hot broiler for 2–3 minutes until golden brown. Serve hot.

CREOLE GUMBO

Served over boiled rice and packed full of tasty chicken, seafood, and vegetables, spicy gumbo is a feast in itself. For a fun, informal meal with friends, nothing could be easier.

Serves 4

¼ cup canola oil	¼ tsp cayenne pepper
⅓ cup all-purpose flour	Salt and freshly ground pepper
1 onion, finely chopped	1–1½ lbs skinless and boneless chicken thighs, cut into chunks
1 red bell pepper, cored, seeded, and finely chopped	½ lb okra, thinly sliced
2 garlic cloves, minced	½ lb medium-size raw shrimp, peeled, deveined, and chopped
14-oz can crushed tomatoes	¼ tsp filé powder (see box, right)
5 cups hot chicken stock	Boiled rice and chopped scallions for serving
2 tbs chopped fresh parsley	
1 tsp dried thyme	

GUMBO

A cross between a soup and a stew, a good gumbo is thick with ingredients and pungent with herbs and spices. There are three secrets to making good gumbo – starting with a richly colored roux, thickening with okra, and finishing with a good quality filé powder. The roux should cook for at least 15 minutes to give the gumbo a rich, nutty color and flavor, and some Creole cooks cook their roux for up to an hour and more. Filé powder, a seasoning made from ground sassafras leaves, thickens the gumbo in addition to the okra, and gives it its unique woody flavor. It's added off the heat so it thickens without toughening.

1 Heat the oil in a large heavy pan, sprinkle in the flour, and cook over gentle heat, stirring constantly, for 15–20 minutes to make a rich, nut-brown roux. Add the onion, red pepper, and garlic and sauté, stirring frequently, for 5 minutes or until soft.

2 Add the tomatoes and stir well to mix, then pour in the stock and add the herbs, cayenne, and salt and pepper to taste. Bring to a boil and add the chicken, then cover and simmer for 20 minutes, stirring occasionally.

3 Add the okra and simmer for 10 minutes. Add the shrimp and simmer for 2–3 minutes until pink. Off the heat, add the filé powder and stir until the gumbo thickens slightly. Taste for seasoning. Serve hot over boiled rice, sprinkled with scallions.

TUSCAN BEAN SOUP

With its olive oil, vegetables, beans, and herbs, this country-style soup evokes the aromas and flavors of the region of Tuscany in northern Italy. Serve it with crusty Italian bread and a bottle of good Chianti – the region's most famous red wine.

Serves 4

¾ lb dried white cannellini beans, soaked in cold water overnight	2 garlic cloves, finely chopped
2 onions, finely chopped	¼ lb thick-cut pancetta (see box, right), diced
2 carrots, finely chopped	1 cup crushed sieved tomatoes (page 40)
2 celery stalks, finely chopped	
2 sprigs fresh thyme	Salt and freshly ground pepper
2 bay leaves, torn	¼ cup chopped fresh parsley
⅓ cup virgin olive oil	

ITALIAN PANCETTA

*This unsmoked, salt-cured pork is widely used as a flavoring ingredient in Italian cooking. Looking very similar to bacon, it is available either round or oblong in shape at Italian delis and specialty markets. Italian cooks dice or slice pancetta into thin strips and use it to add a subtle saltiness to sauces, soups, and stuffings, and it is always included in the classic Italian **soffrito**, which is used as a foundation for so many sauces, soups, casseroles, and stews. Very thinly sliced, best quality pancetta is often eaten uncooked with other cold meats as part of an antipasto.*

1 Drain the beans and place in a large pan with half the onions, carrots, and celery, and the thyme and bay leaves. Pour in 6 cups water and bring to a boil. Cover and simmer for 1 hour or until the beans are tender.

2 Heat ¼ cup oil in a large pan and add the remaining onions, carrots, and celery with the garlic and pancetta. Cook gently for 5 minutes or until the vegetables soften. Add the tomatoes and plenty of salt and pepper and simmer for a few minutes.

3 Purée one-third of the beans and liquid in a blender or food processor. Add to the vegetables with the whole beans and liquid and heat through, adding water if too thick. Add the parsley and taste for seasoning. Serve hot, drizzled with the remaining oil.

COUNTRY VEGETABLE SOUP

Nourishing vegetable soup is tucked away under a crisp, golden pastry lid. If short of time, serve the soup without the pastry and with crusty bread instead.

Serves 4

3 tbs canola oil	2 tbs wholewheat flour
2 celery stalks, thinly sliced	3½ cups hot vegetable stock
4 carrots, thinly sliced	6 ozs mushrooms, thinly sliced
3 leeks, thickly sliced	¼ cup chopped fresh parsley
¾ lb rutabaga or turnip, diced	½ lb frozen puff pastry, thawed
Salt and freshly ground pepper	Beaten egg for glazing

Seasonal choice
In summer, use squash instead of the rutabaga or turnip.

1 Heat the oil in a large pan and add the vegetables, except the mushrooms, and salt and pepper to taste. Cover and cook gently, stirring occasionally, for 10 minutes. Sprinkle in the flour and stir for 1–2 minutes, then pour in the stock and bring to a boil.

2 Add the mushrooms, cover, and simmer for 10 minutes. Pour into 4 soup bowls, stir in the parsley, and leave until cold. Meanwhile, roll out the pastry on a floured surface and cut out 4 lids for the bowls and 4 strips long enough to fit around the rims.

3 Stick the pastry strips onto the rims of the bowls with water. Brush the strips with water and press the lids on top. Decorate with pastry trimmings and brush with beaten egg to glaze, then bake in a preheated 400°F oven for 30 minutes.

SPICED LENTIL AND CHORIZO SOUP

Colorful and tasty, this meaty Mexican-style soup may be served topped with spoonfuls of chilled sour cream or plain yogurt – a cooling contrast for a hot and spicy meal.

Serves 4

2 tbs virgin olive oil	1 large red bell pepper, cored, seeded, and finely chopped
10 ozs chorizo sausage, (see box, right), sliced on the diagonal	½ lb red lentils
2 garlic cloves, roughly chopped	About 5 cups hot chicken stock
1 fresh or dried red chili, seeds removed, roughly chopped	Salt and freshly ground pepper
1 onion, finely chopped	

CHORIZO

This dark red, coarsely textured sausage can be made from fresh pork, in which case it is Mexican, or smoked pork, in which case it is Spanish. Either can be used in this soup, and both are cooked in the same way.

*There are many different varieties of chorizo, some more highly spiced than others; some smoked varieties are used more as a slicing sausage than for cooking. To make this soup even spicier, you could use **chorizo piccante**, which is seasoned with ground red chilies.*

1 Heat the oil in a large pan and add the chorizo. Sauté over moderate to high heat, stirring constantly, until the chorizo is crispy. Take the pan from the heat and remove the chorizo from the oil with a slotted spoon. Drain the chorizo on paper towels.

2 Pound the garlic and chili to a paste with a mortar and pestle. Return the pan to the heat. Add the paste along with the onion and half the bell pepper. Cook over low heat for 5 minutes or until the vegetables soften.

3 Add the lentils, 5 cups stock, and salt and pepper to taste, and bring to a boil. Cover and simmer for 15 minutes or until the lentils are tender, adding more stock if too thick. Add the chorizo and remaining bell pepper, and taste for seasoning. Serve hot.

JAMAICAN BEEF PEPPERPOT

Named for its pepperiness, pepperpot soup is hot and spicy, a filling meal for when you're really hungry. For the best flavor, make it the day before serving.

Serves 4

2 tbs canola oil	6 cups hot beef stock
1 onion, finely chopped	2 tbs tomato paste
2 garlic cloves, finely chopped	½ tsp dried thyme
2 green bell peppers, cored, seeded, and finely chopped	¼–½ tsp hot pepper sauce (see box)
	Salt and freshly ground pepper
4 slices bacon, diced	
1 lb boneless beef shank, diced	1 lb sweet potatoes, peeled and diced
2 tbs all-purpose flour	Chopped fresh thyme for garnish

HOT PEPPER SAUCE

The best known, and perhaps the hottest of pepper sauces, has to be Tabasco. First made in the mid-1800s on Avery Island in Louisiana, this famous sauce is still produced by the McIlhenny family according to the original recipe. Tabasco chilies and salt are ground to a mash, fermented for 3 years, then mixed with vinegar, churned, and filtered.

1 Heat the oil in a large pan and add the onion, garlic, and green pepper. Cook gently for 10 minutes or until softened. Add the bacon and beef, increase the heat, and cook, stirring constantly, until the beef is browned on all sides.

2 Sprinkle in the flour and stir to mix, then gradually pour in 5 cups stock and bring to a boil. Lower the heat, and add the tomato paste and thyme, with hot pepper sauce and salt and pepper to taste. Cover and simmer, stirring occasionally, for 1 hour.

3 Add the sweet potato and the remaining stock and bring back to a boil. Continue cooking for 30 minutes or until the beef and sweet potato are tender. Taste for seasoning, add more pepper sauce if you like, and sprinkle with thyme before serving.

CLAM CHOWDERS

Here are two famous American soups, one fresh and piquant, the other creamy and rich. Despite these differences in flavor and color, they are both based on a similar method.

NEW ENGLAND CLAM CHOWDER

Serves 4

3 dozen clams

¼ lb thick-cut bacon, diced

1 onion, diced

2 potatoes, peeled and diced

2 tbs all-purpose flour

2½ cups milk

Salt and freshly ground pepper

½ cup light cream

Paprika for garnish

1 Shuck the clams (see box, right). Measure the juice, and add enough water to make 2½ cups. Roughly chop the clams.

2 Cook the bacon in a large heavy pan until crispy. Drain on paper towels. Add the onion and potatoes to the fat in the pan and cook for 5 minutes. Add the flour and stir for 1 minute.

3 Add the clam juice, milk, and salt and pepper to taste. Simmer for 20 minutes. Add the clams and simmer gently for 5 minutes, then add the cream. Serve hot, sprinkled with the bacon and garnished with paprika.

MANHATTAN CLAM CHOWDER

Serves 4

3 dozen clams

¼ lb thick-cut bacon, diced

1 onion, diced

2 potatoes, peeled and diced

28-oz can peeled plum tomatoes, chopped, with their juice

½ tsp thyme leaves

Salt and freshly ground pepper

Chopped fresh parsley and thyme sprigs for garnish

1 Shuck the clams (see box, right). Measure the juice, and add enough water to make 2½ cups. Roughly chop the clams.

2 Cook the bacon in a large heavy pan until crispy. Drain on paper towels. Add the onion and potatoes to the fat in the pan and cook for 5 minutes.

3 Add the clam juice, tomatoes, thyme, and salt and pepper to taste. Simmer for 20 minutes. Add the clams and simmer gently for 5 minutes. Serve hot, sprinkled with the bacon and garnished with parsley and thyme.

SHUCKING CLAMS

The best way to shuck uncooked clams is with a special clam or oyster knife.

Place a strainer over a bowl. Hold the clam over the strainer, insert the blade of the clam or oyster knife between the shell halves, and work it around from one side to the other.

Open out the shell and detach the clam by loosening the muscle with the tip of the knife. Tip the clam and juice into the strainer.

MINESTRONE

Italian minestrone is the quintessential main course soup. This version combines fresh vegetables with pasta and beans in a flavorful tomato broth. Serve with hot ciabatta for a substantial and satisfying meal.

Serves 4

3 tbs virgin olive oil	Salt and freshly ground pepper
2–3 celery stalks, finely chopped	14-oz can cannellini beans, drained
3 carrots, finely chopped	1 cup short-cut pasta
1 onion, finely chopped	1 cup fresh or frozen shelled peas
¼ lb bacon, diced	2 tbs chopped fresh flat-leaf parsley
28-oz can peeled plum tomatoes	Parsley sprigs and Parmesan curls (page 94) for garnish
4 cups hot chicken or vegetable stock	

Seasonal choice
Use ½ lb shredded green cabbage in winter, instead of the peas.

MINESTRONE ALLA MILANESE

*This fresh vegetable soup from Milan in northern Italy is made with dried cannellini beans and pasta, but there are numerous variations, some with rice instead of pasta, others with potatoes, cabbage, and green beans rather than the peas used here. The Milanese cook uses whatever is on hand on the day, so no two minestrone soups are alike. A different, richer kind of minestrone is **minestrone alla Genovese**, which is served with a generous spoonful or two of pesto stirred in at the end and a liberal sprinkling of freshly grated pecorino cheese.*

1 Heat the oil in a large pan and add the celery, carrots, onion, and bacon. Cook over gentle heat, stirring constantly, for about 5 minutes until the vegetables are softened but not colored.

2 Add the tomatoes, stock, and salt and pepper to taste and bring to a boil. Cover and simmer gently, stirring occasionally, for 20 minutes or until the vegetables are very soft.

3 Add the beans, pasta, and peas. Cover and simmer for 20 minutes. Stir in the parsley, then taste for seasoning. Serve hot, garnished with parsley sprigs and Parmesan curls.

CHICKEN AND LEEK SOUP

Pieces of tender chicken and rings of leek are combined in a flavorful broth to make this traditional homey soup. Slivers of pitted prunes are the secret ingredient, adding a touch of sweetness and color.

C O C K - A - L E E K I E

*Chicken and leek soup, better known as cock-a-leekie, is thought to have originated in Scotland, but there are many versions all over the British Isles, particularly in Wales and the West country. The original cock would have been an old farmyard rooster, too tough to roast, but made tender and tasty by long slow simmering with water, vegetables, and flavorings. The broth and vegetables of cock-a-leekie are traditionally eaten as a first course, then the meat is cut up and eaten separately as a main course – rather like the French **pot-au-feu**. In this recipe they are served together to make a hearty one-dish meal.*

Serves 4

2½–3-lb chicken	3–4 leeks, total weight about 1 lb, thinly sliced
1 small onion, peeled and studded with 1–2 cloves	¼ cup long-grain rice
1 carrot, quartered lengthwise	8 prunes, pitted and cut into bite-size pieces
1 bouquet garni	Chopped fresh parsley for garnish
Salt and freshly ground pepper	

Finishing touches

Top the soup with the finely shredded green parts of the leeks or with finely chopped toasted almonds instead of chopped parsley.

1 Put the chicken in a large pot and add the onion, carrot, bouquet garni, 1 tsp salt, and pepper to taste. Cover with cold water and bring to a boil. Skim off any scum, cover, and simmer for 45 minutes. Let cool.

2 Remove the chicken from the stock. Take the meat off the bones and shred into bite-size pieces. Discard the skin. Strain the stock; there should be 6 cups. Make up the volume with water if necessary. Bring to a boil in a clean pan.

3 Add the leeks, rice, and prunes. Cover and simmer for 10 minutes or until the leeks and rice are tender. Add the chicken, heat through, and taste for seasoning. Serve hot, sprinkled with parsley.

HOT AND SOUR SOUP

This Chinese soup makes a good winter main course because the hot and sour flavors have a substantial warming effect. Serve it Asian style – with chopsticks for the chicken and vegetables, and soup spoons on the side for the broth.

RICE WINE

*Mellow-tasting and richly colored, Chinese rice wine should not be confused with Japanese rice wine or **sake**, which is colorless. Chinese rice wine is made from glutinous rice, water, and yeast, and is used extensively in Chinese cooking – just a spoonful or two added to soups, sauces, and stir-fries helps impart an authentic Chinese flavor. Available in bottles from Chinese and other Asian supermarkets, it is not expensive and will keep for a long time at cool room temperature as long as the lid is screwed on tightly. If you are unable to find rice wine, dry or medium-dry sherry can be used instead.*

Serves 4

1 tb canola oil	Freshly ground pepper
2 eggs, beaten with salt and freshly ground pepper	1 bunch scallions, thinly sliced on the diagonal
2 15-oz cans chicken consommé (page 84)	2 carrots, grated
2 tbs rice wine (see box, right)	About ¾ lb shredded cooked chicken
2 tbs soy sauce	Shredded fresh coriander (cilantro, page 47) for garnish
2 tbs white wine vinegar	
1 tsp sugar	

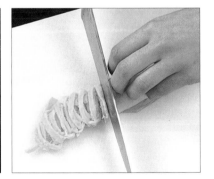

1 Heat the oil in an omelet pan, add the eggs, and allow to run in the pan. Cook just until set, lifting up the edge so the unset egg runs underneath. Turn over and cook the other side. Slide onto a board, and roll up. Let cool, seam-side down.

2 Pour the consommé into a large pan. Add the rice wine or sherry, soy sauce, wine vinegar, sugar, and pepper to taste. Heat gently, add the scallions and carrots, and simmer for 5 minutes until just tender. Stir in the chicken and heat through.

3 Cut the omelet crosswise into fine shreds. Taste the soup, and add more soy sauce, wine vinegar, or sugar if you like. Ladle the soup into warmed bowls and scatter with the omelet shreds. Garnish with coriander and serve at once.

ITALIAN CLAM AND PASTA SOUP

Juicy red tomatoes flecked with herbs combine with tiny pasta shells and clams in this exquisite-tasting soup. Serve with hot herb focaccia.

Serves 4

2 tbs virgin olive oil	1 tsp sugar
1 large onion, finely chopped	Salt and freshly ground pepper
2 garlic cloves, minced	2–3 ozs small-cut pasta
14-oz can crushed tomatoes with Italian herbs	2 5-oz jars clams in natural juice
3–3½ cups hot fish or chicken stock	¼ cup shredded fresh basil (page 94)
1 tb tomato paste	A few fresh clams in their shells for garnish (optional)

BABY CLAMS

Jars of baby clams are very convenient for soup-making because they take all the hard work out of shucking, and if they are bottled in their natural juices these can be used in the broth to add extra flavor.
If you prefer to use fresh clams in this soup, however, you can use any of the hardshell varieties such as littleneck, cherrystone, or chowder clams, and you will need about 1 dozen of them. Shuck the clams following the directions in the box on page 71, and reserve the liquid from the shells, then roughly chop the clams if they are large, and add them with their liquid at the beginning of step 3.

1 Heat the oil in a large pan, add the onion, and cook gently for 5 minutes or until softened. Add the garlic, tomatoes, 3 cups stock, the tomato paste, sugar, and salt and pepper to taste. Bring to a boil, cover, and simmer for 15 minutes.

2 Add the pasta to the soup and bring back to a boil. Simmer, uncovered, for about 10 minutes until the pasta is just al dente (tender but firm to the bite), stirring frequently to prevent the pasta from sticking.

3 Add the clams and their juice to the soup and heat through for a few minutes, adding more stock if too thick. Taste for seasoning. Serve hot, sprinkled with the basil, and garnished with clams in their shells if you like.

SINGAPORE LAKSA

Known locally as *laksa lemak*, or coconut soup, this exotic mixture of shrimp, noodles, and vegetables is rich with coconut milk and piquant with spices. Serve it as a one-dish meal like the Singaporeans do, with crispy shrimp crackers on the side.

COCONUT MILK

For convenience and speed, canned coconut milk is best, but it is expensive, and not always easy to find. To make your own, put 2 cups unsweetened shredded or freshly grated coconut in a bowl and pour 2½ cups boiling water over it. Let stand for 30 minutes, then tip the mixture into a strainer set over a bowl, and press on the coconut to extract as much "milk" as possible. The coconut can be used twice in this way to make a thick coconut milk or "cream," and then a thinner milk. Use the thick milk for making Singapore Laksa and refrigerate the thin milk for another use.

Serves 4–6

½–¾ lb unpeeled large raw shrimp	1½ cups coconut milk (see box, right)
5 cups hot chicken stock	1 tb soy sauce or Thai fish sauce
2 tbs canola oil	2–3 ozs dried Chinese egg noodles
2-inch piece fresh ginger root, crushed	2 carrots, cut into matchsticks
2 garlic cloves, finely chopped	¼ lb green beans, halved crosswise
¼–½ tsp turmeric	2 cups bean sprouts
¼–½ tsp hot chili powder	Fresh coriander (cilantro, page 47) for garnish

1 Put the shrimp and 2½ cups stock in a wok. Bring to a boil and simmer for 1–2 minutes until the shrimp turn pink. Remove with a slotted spoon and let cool. Strain the liquid and skim off any scum. Peel and devein the shrimp and cut each one into 2–3 pieces.

2 Heat the oil in the wok, add the ginger, garlic, and spices, and cook gently for 5 minutes or until fragrant. Add the shrimp liquid and the remaining stock, the coconut milk, and soy or fish sauce. Bring to a boil and simmer for 10 minutes.

3 Add the noodles in pieces. Simmer for 5 minutes, then add the carrots and beans and simmer for 2–3 minutes. Add the shrimp and bean sprouts, then taste and add more soy or fish sauce if you like. Serve hot, garnished with coriander.

MOROCCAN LAMB SOUP WITH COUSCOUS

This soup-stew from North Africa is full of wonderful ingredients and flavors. Make it ahead of time and let it cool. On reheating, its flavor will be more intense.

Serves 4

2 tbs canola oil	6 cups hot chicken stock
1 onion, finely chopped	Salt and freshly ground pepper
1–2 garlic cloves, minced	2 carrots, finely diced
2 tsps ground coriander or cumin	1–2 parsnips, finely diced
1 tsp chili powder	2 zucchini, finely diced
1 tsp turmeric	¼ lb couscous (see box, right) for serving
1 lb lamb fillet, finely diced	
2 tbs tomato paste	Fresh coriander (cilantro, page 47) leaves for garnish

1 Heat the oil in a large pan, add the onion, and cook gently for 5 minutes or until softened but not colored. Add the garlic and spices and cook for 5 minutes, stirring frequently, until the spices smell fragrant.

2 Add the lamb and stir until well coated with the spice mixture, then add the tomato paste, stock, 1 tsp salt, and pepper to taste. Cover and simmer gently, stirring occasionally, for 1 hour or until the lamb is just tender.

3 Add the vegetables and a little water if too thick, and simmer for 20 minutes or until the lamb is very tender. Taste for seasoning. Divide the prepared couscous among warmed bowls, top with the soup, and garnish with coriander. Serve at once.

BEEF BROTH WITH HERB DUMPLINGS

The simple addition of homemade herb dumplings quickly turns canned consommé into a special dish, ideal for a light lunch or supper.

Serves 4

¾ cup all-purpose flour	Salt and freshly ground pepper
½ cup grated lard or ¼ cup vegetable shortening	2 15-oz cans beef consommé (see box, right)
2 tbs chopped mixed fresh herbs, plus extra for garnish	¼ cup Madeira (page 12) or port

Finishing touches
Instead of mixed herbs, sprinkle the finished soup with finely grated orange or lemon zest.

CONSOMME

This is a thin, flavorful broth, generally made from beef, chicken, or fish simmered with aromatic vegetables and flavorings, then clarified with whisked egg whites until it is crystal clear. In classic French cuisine, consommé is served hot, garnished with slivers of meat or vegetables, pasta, rice, tapioca, poached egg, or tiny croûtons, or it can be served chilled and jellied. Although consommé can be made at home, the method is rather time-consuming and not particularly easy. Canned consommé both looks and tastes very good, and can be easily dressed up with the addition of a few simple ingredients, as in this recipe and on page 76.

1 Make the dumplings: mix together the flour, lard, and 2 tbs herbs, with salt and pepper to taste. Stir in about 3 tbs cold water until the mixture holds together. Form into 12 balls.

2 Pour the consommé into a large pot, add the Madeira or port, and heat through gently. Drop in the dumplings and simmer for 10 minutes or until cooked.

3 Taste the soup and adjust the seasoning, then ladle into warmed bowls, dividing the dumplings equally among them. Sprinkle with additional chopped fresh herbs and serve at once.

MEXICAN THREE BEAN SOUP

This spicy hot soup tastes good served with crisp tortilla chips on the side. Ice-cold beer would make a cooling accompaniment.

Serves 4–6

2 red bell peppers	1 tsp ground cumin
14-oz can red kidney beans	½–1 tsp hot chili powder (see box, right)
14-oz can white cannellini beans	
14-oz can green flageolet beans	4 cups hot chicken or vegetable stock
2 tbs virgin olive oil	
1 onion, finely chopped	Salt and freshly ground pepper
2 garlic cloves, finely chopped	¼ cup chopped fresh coriander (cilantro, page 47)
2 celery stalks, diced	¼ cup sour cream

CHILI POWDER

Take care when using chili powder because brands vary enormously. Pure chili powder is very finely ground chilies, and is searingly hot. Most brands labeled "chili powder" are not pure chili, but a blend of ground spices, dried herbs, and salt, with ground chilies among them. A typical blend includes garlic, onion, cumin, allspice, oregano, and salt, all of which have a mellowing effect on the chilies and are the traditional flavorings in **chili con carne**. *In authentic Mexican cooking, pure chili powder is most often used, but for this bean soup recipe a mild mixture is preferable.*

1 Broil the peppers until their skins are charred black on all sides, then place in a plastic bag. Seal the bag and let the peppers cool, then peel off the skins. Chop the peppers, discarding the cores and seeds.

2 Drain and rinse the beans. Heat the oil in a large pan and add the onion, garlic, and celery. Cook gently for 5 minutes or until the onion softens. Add the cumin and chili powder to taste and stir for 1–2 minutes. Add the stock and bring to a boil.

3 Add the beans and salt and pepper to taste, cover, and simmer for 10 minutes. Add the chopped peppers and coriander, heat through, and taste for seasoning. Serve hot, garnished with sour cream and more freshly ground black pepper.

BORSCHT

In this rich Russian-style soup, strips of beef and fresh beet are cooked until tender in a sweet-sour broth. Sour cream and puff pastry crescents make authentic finishing touches.

Serves 4

½ lb chuck steak	1 lb fresh beet
1 small onion, peeled and studded with 1–2 cloves	2 tbs red wine vinegar
1 carrot, sliced	2 tbs tomato paste
2 celery stalks, roughly chopped	1 tsp sugar
1 bouquet garni	Sour cream and fresh dill sprigs for garnish
Salt and freshly ground pepper	
2 beef bouillon cubes, crumbled	Puff pastry crescents (see box, right) for serving

PUFF PASTRY CRESCENTS

The traditional accompaniments for beet soup are **piroshki**, *little pastry turnovers filled with a tasty ground meat or vegetable mixture. Puff pastry crescents make a quick and easy alternative with a similar shape. Simply roll out ¼ lb commercial puff pastry on a lightly floured surface and cut it into crescent shapes with a small cookie cutter.*

Place the crescents on a dampened baking sheet, score in a small diamond pattern with the tip of a sharp knife, and brush with beaten egg. Bake in a preheated 400°F oven for 5–8 minutes until puffed, crisp, and golden. Cool slightly on a wire rack before serving.

1 Put the beef in a pan with the onion, carrot, celery, bouquet garni, 1 tsp salt, and pepper to taste. Add 3½ cups water and 1 stock cube, and bring to a boil. Skim, cover, and simmer for 1 hour or until the beef is just tender. Remove the beef and let cool.

2 Peel the beet and cut into matchsticks. Cut the beef into matchsticks. Strain the stock and pour into a clean pan. Add 3 cups water and the remaining stock cube, the vinegar, tomato paste, sugar, and plenty of pepper. Bring to a boil, stirring.

3 Add the beef and beet to the boiling stock. Cover and simmer for 45 minutes or until both are tender. Taste for seasoning. Serve hot, garnished with sour cream and dill, with puff pastry crescents on the side.

SUMMER SQUASH SOUP

This Provençal soup uses the best of summer ingredients – squash, plum tomatoes, and fava beans. When combined with the pungent flavors of olive oil, garlic, and basil, the aroma of the finished soup is reminiscent of hot Mediterranean summers.

Serves 4

1 lb ripe plum tomatoes	Salt and freshly ground pepper
3 tbs virgin olive oil	5 cups hot chicken or vegetable stock
1 large onion, finely chopped	
2 garlic cloves, minced	½ cup fresh or frozen shelled fava beans
1 lb summer squash (see box, right), diced	2 ozs farfalle or other medium-cut pasta
2 medium potatoes, peeled and diced	½ cup grated Parmesan cheese
2 heaping tbs chopped sun-dried tomatoes in oil	¼ cup coarsely chopped fresh basil (page 94) for garnish

SUMMER SQUASH

Soft-skinned, young, and tender, these include green and yellow zucchini, white and pale green pattypan squash, scalloped squash, and yellow straightnecks. All of these make good soup, so you can choose whichever you prefer. Leave the skins on for maximum flavor and color, but scrub them gently with a vegetable brush under cold running water to remove any surface dirt before dicing. Some cooks sprinkle sliced or diced squash with salt before cooking and let the squash stand for 30 minutes or so to draw out the bitter juices, but this is unnecessary with mild flavored summer squash.

1 Cover the tomatoes with boiling water, drain, and immerse in cold water. Drain again, peel off the skins, and dice the flesh. Heat the oil in a large pan and add the onion. Cook over gentle heat, stirring constantly, for 5 minutes or until soft.

2 Add the garlic and diced vegetables to the pan with the sun-dried tomatoes and salt and pepper to taste. Cover and cook gently for 10 minutes, shaking the pan frequently. Pour in the stock and simmer for 15 minutes or until the vegetables are tender.

3 Add the fava beans and pasta and simmer for 10 minutes or until the pasta is al dente (tender but firm to the bite). Remove from the heat, add half the Parmesan, and taste for seasoning. Serve hot, sprinkled with basil and the remaining Parmesan.

FRUIT SOUPS

Scandinavian-style fruit soups are refreshing on hot summer days, and perfect to kick off a barbecue in the backyard. They can double up as desserts too, making them well worth having in your culinary repertoire.

SUGAR PLUM SOUP

Serves 4

1 cup fruity white wine

2 tbs sugar

2 tbs brandy

1 cinnamon stick

Zest and juice of ½ orange

1 lb red plums, halved and pitted

½ cup sour cream

Ground cinnamon for garnish

1 Gently heat 2 cups water, the wine, and sugar in a pan until the sugar dissolves. Add the brandy, cinnamon stick, and orange zest and bring to a boil. Simmer for 10 minutes or until syrupy. Discard the cinnamon stick and orange zest.

2 Add the plums to the sugar syrup. Bring to a boil again, then cover and simmer, stirring occasionally, for 10 minutes or until the fruit is soft.

3 Work the soup in a blender or food processor until smooth, then strain into a bowl. Let cool, then stir in the orange juice and sour cream until evenly mixed. Chill for at least 4 hours. Dust each serving with cinnamon.

ICED BERRY SOUP

Serves 4

1 cup fruity white wine

2 tbs sugar

2 tbs kirsch or vodka

Zest and juice of ½ lemon

1 lb raspberries

1 cup crème fraîche (page 39)

1 Gently heat 2 cups water, the wine, and sugar in a pan until the sugar dissolves. Add the kirsch or vodka and the lemon zest and bring to a boil. Simmer for 10 minutes or until syrupy. Discard the lemon zest.

2 Add the raspberries to the sugar syrup. Bring to a boil again, then cover and simmer, stirring occasionally, for 10 minutes or until the fruit is soft.

3 Pour the soup into a blender or food processor, add about three-quarters of the crème fraîche, and work until smooth. Strain into a bowl. Let cool, stir in the lemon juice, and chill for at least 4 hours. Garnish each serving with some of the remaining crème fraîche.

MINTY MELON SOUP

Serves 4

1 cup fruity white wine

2 tbs sugar

1 small handful fresh mint sprigs

2 lbs cantaloupe melon, skin, seeds, and fibers removed, cut into chunks

1 cup light cream

Fresh mint leaves for garnish

1 Gently heat 3 cups water, the wine, and sugar in a pan until the sugar dissolves. Add the mint sprigs and bring to a boil. Simmer for 10 minutes or until syrupy. Discard the mint sprigs.

2 Add the melon to the sugar syrup. Bring to a boil again, then cover and simmer, stirring occasionally, for 10 minutes or until the melon is soft.

3 Work the soup in a blender or food processor until smooth, then strain into a bowl. Let cool, then stir in the cream. Chill for at least 4 hours. Garnish each serving with a fresh mint leaf.

FINISHING TOUCHES

Simple last-minute touches transform plain soups into feasts for the eye. Match garnishes to soups with similar flavors.

Citrus Julienne
Remove the zest (colored skin) of citrus fruit with a vegetable peeler and cut into very thin strips. Blanch in boiling water for 1–2 minutes, rinse in cold water, and pat dry. Pile delicately in center of soups.

Parmesan Curls
Hold a block of fresh Parmesan cheese firmly in one hand. Using a vegetable peeler in the other hand, shave off thin slivers of cheese, which will curl slightly at the ends. Arrange in center of soups.

Fines Herbes
Pile herb leaves on a board and cut into small pieces. Holding the tip of the knife against the board, rock the blade back and forth across the herbs until finely chopped. Scatter over soups, or pile in little clumps.

Spice Dust
Put whole dried spices, such as peppercorns, allspice berries, coriander, cumin, and caraway seeds, in a mortar and pound to a powdery dust with a pestle. Sprinkle over soups very sparingly.

Basil Shreds
Remove leaves from basil stems and stack several leaves on top of one another on a board. Roll up into a cigar shape, then cut across into fine shreds. Group shreds together on top of soups, or scatter them loosely for a more casual effect.

Crunchy Nuts
Spread shelled sliced or chopped nuts, such as almonds, pecans, or hazelnuts, on a baking sheet. Toast in a preheated 350°F oven for 6–8 minutes, stirring occasionally so they brown evenly. Sprinkle over soups just before serving.

CREAM DECORATIONS

Smooth-textured soups look stunning with the addition of pretty patterns of cream. They can be subtle and light, bold and dramatic, plain or fancy. Once you know how, you can experiment with your own designs.

First Things First
For best results, use chilled heavy or whipping cream and lightly whip it with a balloon whisk until it just holds its shape. This allows the cream to sit on the surface of the soup without sinking.

Simple Spiral
Drizzle cream from the tip of a teaspoon, starting in the center of the soup and working outward in a spiral. You can make the spiral small or large, as you like.

Pinwheel
Put a spoonful of cream in the center of the soup. With the tip of a small sharp knife, draw the cream out from the center in curved strokes.

Necklace of Hearts
Drip cream from a teaspoon to make a circle of small dots, either around the edge of the soup or in the center. Draw the tip of a small sharp knife through the dots to join them together.

Saucy Squiggle
Drizzle cream from the tip of a teaspoon in a freeform squiggly pattern. When the squiggle is made, lift the spoon up quickly to finish neatly.

Fleur de Lis
Drizzle a circle of cream from the tip of a teaspoon. Draw the tip of a small sharp knife through the cream at regular intervals, first inward, then outward.

RECIPE INDEX

ACKNOWLEDGMENTS

Photographer's assistant Sid Sideris
Food preparation Maddalena Bastianelli
Production consultant Lorraine Baird
Index Madeline Weston
Illustrations Jo Hamill